T0132437

Princess Yellow Hair and the Troll

Written by:

RubySue

Illustrations by: Lyle Jakosalem

Print information available on the last page

Rev. date: 02/19/2016

To order additional copies of this book, contact:
Xlibris
1-888-795-4274
www.Xlibris.com
Orders@Xlibris.com

$\mathcal{O}$nce there was a little girl whose eyes were as blue as the sky and whose hair was a golden as the sunlight. She was sweet and kind to everyone she met and liked to do kind deeds. Everyone called her Princess Yellow Hair as she skipped through the village with her golden hair flowing in the wind.

Princess Yellow Hair was kind and sweet and had many friends. She enjoyed doing acts of kindness for others in her village and taking tiny delicate violets to her mama who worked hard to keep up with all the household chores while Daddy was out working.

Beautiful purple violets grew wild by the tracks at the edge of the village. These were Mama's favorite flowers, but a troll lived near the tracks and scared people away. Mama had warned her cheerful little princess to stay away from there, but the brave little girl loved giving violets to her mama and continued to pick them from time to time.

One day, when Princess Yellow Hair was picking violets, a troll suddenly appeared on the other side of the tracks. "Who's picking my violets?" boomed the troll.

"Well, it's me, Princess Yellow Hair," replied a sweet little voice. "These are my mama's favorites, and I'm going to give them to her."

"NO!" roared the troll. "You CANNOT pick those violets!"

"I can. And I will," replied the brave little princess. "These are wild flowers, and they belong to everyone." By now, she had a handful of the pretty little purple flowers for her mama.

"This is enough," said Princess Yellow Hair with a smile as she skipped off with her golden hair flowing in the wind. She left behind a very perplexed and angry troll.

He wondered why he hadn't scared her away. People were always afraid of him. *"That's a brave princess,"* he thought to himself as he kicked the ground and headed back to his cabin in the woods.

Mama loved the flowers. "Thank you," she said as she kissed the little princess on the forehead. "These are so lovely!" Mama put the violets in a vase of water on the table. Once again, Mama warned Princess Yellow Hair to beware of the troll at the edge of the village and to be careful picking flowers so close to the tracks where he lived. After all, the troll owned all the land outside the village. It was his inheritance from many generations before him, and he did not like anyone coming near him or his property. In fact, he had been so mean and grumpy for so long that everyone had forgotten he had a name. They just called him Troll.

"I'm not afraid of a silly ole troll," declared the princess. "Those violets belong to everyone, and he should stop trying to scare people."

Mama explained that the troll had lived there for a long time, and he did not want to see progress come to the village. The tracks were being laid to connect their village with other villages and would make travel time a lot faster if a train could pass through this area, connecting the east villages with the west villages. The troll had scared the workers away and had stopped the progress.

"Hmmmm." The little golden-haired princess sighed as she pondered on what Mama had just told her.

As the days past, Princess Yellow Hair went about doing good deeds. She took cookies to the widow and her children down the street. She sat and read stories to her aging grandmother. She helped the boy next door sweep up pine needles from his yard. She played games with the small children in the neighborhood. And she helped her mama clean the house. Her sweet smile and soft voice encouraged all those around her.

When Mama's violets needed replacing, Princess Yellow Hair skipped off to where they grew wild by the tracks. She was on the lookout for the troll. She didn't see him, so she hummed a little tune as she set about her task of picking the lovely little flowers.

14

"Who's picking my violets?" boomed the loud voice of the troll like a sudden clap of thunder. "You CANNOT pick these violets!" he yelled when he saw the little princess. His bushy white beard shook as his head moved from side to side.

"I can. And I will," replied Princess Yellow Hair as she continued to fill her little hands with the tiny purple flowers. She looked up and smiled a warm smile at the troll.

"NO!" the troll yelled even louder than before, trying to scare her away.

Princess Yellow Hair stood up from her task and held out her hand, reaching across the tracks, and offered the flowers to the surprised troll. "These are for you, Mr. Troll. I think you need some beauty in your life today." A voice as sweet as honey melted the troll's hard heart.

The grumpy old troll was confused at first because he did not have any friends. No one was ever nice to him because he kept scaring them away. But suddenly, his heart was softened by the kind gesture of the little princess, and he didn't want to scare people any more. He reached out and took the bundle of purple flowers from her tiny little hand.

"Thank you," he said shyly.

The little princess gave the troll some of Mama's homemade cookies from her basket and told him that everyone needs friends.

"Tell your village leaders that they can build their tracks. I won't stop them or scare them anymore. My land is ready for progress," said the troll smiling. It was the first time in many years that Bryson Troll had smiled for any reason.

"Oh! Mr. Troll! I knew you could be nice!" squealed the brave little girl. "Just wait and see how great it will be to have friends to talk to." She encouraged him and told him that he had made a good decision.

"Don't forget to take some violets to your mama," said the troll in a kind voice.

So Princess Yellow Hair picked more violets as she hummed a catchy little tune. Soon she and Mr. Troll waved goodbye, and she skipped away with her golden hair blowing in the wind. She promised that she would return another day soon and bring more yummy cookies.

20

Princess Yellow Hair saved the day for her village! The leaders were excited about finishing the tracks that would connect them to other villages. They made friends with the troll who never scared anyone again. In fact, he helped the track builders, and the task went a lot faster. Finally, they could all live in peace and harmony. Even the troll agreed that progress was a good thing!

The brave little Princess Yellow Hair with eyes as blue as the sky, a voice as soft as a summer breeze, a smile as sweet as honey, and hair as golden as the sunlight continued to do good deeds. She loved others, made new friends, took cookies to Mr. Troll, and was helpful and kind each day as she set out on new adventures.

THE END

Dedication

This book is in loving memory of my mama, Doris Cannon Waters, of Roanoke Rapids, NC. I used to pick tiny purple violets for her when I was a little girl. She always smiled and said they were her favorites. They grew wildly by the railroad tracks near our house, and she always warned me to be careful. This story was inspired by memories of her during a recent visit to Roanoke Rapids.

Printed in the United States
By Bookmasters